NATIONAL AUDUBON SOCIETY

The mission of the NATIONAL AUDUBON SOCIETY *is to conserve and restore natural ecosystems, focusing on birds and other wildlife, for the benefit of humanity and the earth's biological diversity.*

With more than 560,000 members and an extensive chapter network, our staff of scientists, educators, lobbyists, lawyers, and policy analysts works to save threatened ecosystems and restore the natural balance of life on our planet. Through our sanctuary system we manage 150,000 acres of critical habitat. *Audubon* magazine, sent to all members, carries outstanding articles and color photography on wildlife, nature, and the environment. We also publish *Field Notes*, a journal reporting bird sightings, and *Audubon Adventures*, a bimonthly children's newsletter reaching 600,000 students.

NATIONAL AUDUBON SOCIETY produces television documentaries and sponsors books, electronic programs, and nature travel to exotic places.

For membership information:

NATIONAL AUDUBON SOCIETY
700 Broadway
New York, NY 10003-9562
212-979-3000

North American Birds of Prey

Text by Clay Sutton
and Richard K. Walton

Alfred A. Knopf, New York

This is a Borzoi Book.
Published by Alfred A. Knopf, Inc.

Prepared and produced by Chanticleer Press, Inc., New York.
Printed and bound by Toppan Printing Co., Ltd., Hong Kong.

Published February 1994
Second Printing, June 1997

Library of Congress Catalog Card Number: 93-21253
ISBN: 0-679-74923-3

Contents

How to Use This Guide

Birds of prey are strong, majestic animals that are fascinating to observe. This guide will help you identify many North American hawks, eagles, falcons, vultures, and owls and learn about their unique habits.

Coverage This book features 56 species of birds of prey, or raptors, that may be observed in North America. They appear in the American Ornithologists' Union's taxonomic order.

Organization There are three parts to this guide: introductory essays; color plates and descriptions; and appendices.

Introduction The three essays that introduce the book serve to define birds of prey, describe the various types, and offer tips on observing and identifying them.

Color Plates This section of photographs and descriptions is divided into two parts. The first presents the 56 species, often showing more than one photograph of each. Most species are represented by a photograph of the male; additional photographs have been included in cases where females or juveniles look markedly different, or where two or more color variations occur. Facing each photograph is a description of the species, beginning with a discussion of its unique or unusual traits. The paragraph labeled

"Identification" gives the adult size and field marks; voice, habitat, and range are described in the sections that follow. Where a second photograph of a species appears, there is an account of its nesting habits.

Breeding range

Winter range

Permanent range

To supplement the range statement, there is a map on which breeding and winter ranges are indicated by diagonal hatching. Where there is an overlap, or wherever a species occurs year-round, the ranges are superimposed. In rare cases, a species occurs so infrequently or in such small numbers that no range map is provided.

Accompanying each account is a small silhouette, designed as an aid in identification. These silhouettes represent general body types but do not necessarily indicate the subtle variations that can occur among species of the same family.

The second part of the color plates presents birds of prey in flight. The accompanying text describes what is distinctive about the flight of various species.

Appendices   A labeled drawing of a bird of prey and a glossary will help you become familiar with terms used to describe bird anatomy and field marks. There is also a list of organizations that sponsor hawk watches in the United States.

7

Introduction to Birds of Prey

This comprehensive volume includes all the birds of prey that occur regularly in North America as well as most of the rarer species that are considered accidental wanderers to our region.

"Bird of prey" is a name applied, in general usage, to any of the carnivorous, or meat-eating, birds that feed through the process of predation. The term raptor is synonymous with bird of prey.

While many birds prey upon other animals—warblers eat insects; herons eat fish; and ravens, crows, and even jays and shrikes often catch and eat other small birds—none is considered to be a true bird of prey. It is the combination of strong legs; powerful feet with sharp, curved talons; and a hooked beak, designed for the "rending of meat," that characterizes the bird of prey. Excellent eyesight and superb powers of flight are also attributes of raptors. The so-called true raptors include the hawk family, the falcon family, the vulture family, and two owl families. (A family is a broad grouping of similar genera.)

Hawks The hawk family, Accipitridae, is made up of diurnal birds of prey (that is, those active during daylight hours), and it includes hawks, kites, ospreys, and eagles. These birds have hooked bills, strong feet, and sharp, curved talons. They have large eyes, and their eyesight is thought to be many times better than that of humans. Females are usually considerably larger than males. Among the Accipitridae, a wide variety of species occurs.

Many hawks can be categorized, in general terms, as being either buteos or accipiters. Buteos are soaring hawks with long, wide wings and short tails. Most prefer open country and feed largely on small rodents, amphibians, and reptiles. They hunt by watching from a perch or soaring in the sky, scanning the ground for prey. Accipiters are forest-dwelling hawks whose short wings and long tails assist them in maneuvering around trees and brush. They also soar, and are occasionally found in open country, especially during migration. Accipiters are "bird hawks," feeding mostly on other birds, which they chase down and catch in flight.

Kites exhibit a wide variety of shapes and lifestyles, but all lack the bony ridge found over the eye of other hawks. Harriers are a type of hawk that seem, superficially, to resemble accipiters. Unlike accipiters, though, harriers are found in open country and hunt with low, coursing flight.

The Osprey, or "fish hawk," one of the most widely distributed raptors in the world, is found in North America, South America, Europe, Asia, Africa, and Australia. Ospreys are exclusively fish-eaters, and they are the only hawks with a reversible outer toe, no doubt an adaptation for catching and eating fish. They have long, rounded claws, equal-length toes, and spicules on the pads of the toes, all of which help them catch and hold slippery fish.

Eagles are very large hawks that exhibit no real structural or behavioral differences from other, smaller hawks. Bald and Golden eagles are among the largest birds of prey, with wingspans up to seven feet. In comparison, the Ferruginous Hawk, the largest buteo, has a 4½-foot wingspan. A male Sharp-shinned Hawk's wingspan may be only 20 inches.

Falcons   Falcons differ considerably from other raptors, and they are in a separate family, Falconidae. These differences are mainly internal, but falcons also have conspicuously toothed and notched bills. They have powerful, taloned feet and large, dark eyes. Long, pointed wings assist them in their rapid flight. Falcons are the fastest raptors; many pursue other birds in swift flight over open country. A male American Kestrel may have a wingspan of only 20 inches, but a female Gyrfalcon may have a span of over four feet. The caracaras are "primitive" falcons—large scavengers that visually resemble buteos.

Vultures The New World vultures, family Cathartidae, are characterized by naked heads, weak feet and claws, and keen eyesight. Some have a strong sense of smell, used for locating food. While very similar in appearance to Old World vultures, they have great structural and internal differences. Not only are the Cathartidae not closely related to other vultures, but they are not very closely related to other birds of prey, either. They are probably most closely allied to storks. All are scavengers and all are excellent at soaring.

The California Condor, with a wingspan of 9½ feet, is one of the largest flying birds in the world. Its numbers reached their peak in the Pleistocene era, over a million years ago.

Owls Owls are clearly birds of prey, but they are not closely related to hawks. Owls are actually most closely allied to the nightjars. Owls and hawks offer an example of convergent evolution, in which species that appear and behave similarly have evolved from widely different ancestors.

Most owls belong to the family Strigidae, the "typical" owl family. They are largely nocturnal (hunting at night), although many are crepuscular (most active at dawn and dusk). A few of the owls are truly diurnal, like hawks. An owl has immovable eyes set in the front of its head and therefore must turn its head to look at anything not directly in front of it. The head can turn up to 270 degrees in either direction. Owls can see perfectly well in daylight but over 50 times better than humans at night. However, many hunt mainly by use of their exceptional hearing. Owls find prey by what is called triangulation. Their ears are set asymmetrically in the head, behind the facial disc, causing different auditory signals to reach each ear. This allows owls to hear "three-dimensionally."

The barn owl family, or Tytonidae, has only one representative in North America. Barn Owls differ from typical owls in having very long legs and a heart-shaped facial disc. An owl's facial disc is thought to reflect sounds to its hidden ears.

Identifying Birds of Prey

Perched high on a dead branch, or sitting quietly at the edge of a road or field, a bird of prey can be identified using knowledge of standard field marks, or patterns of body markings, that are unmistakable or unique to a particular bird. This system of identification was pioneered by Roger Tory Peterson, a renowned ornithologist, and it is especially useful to raptor watchers, who can be frustrated by the many "look-alike" hawk species. Each description in this guide contains an "Identification" section in which such field marks are detailed.

Size
An important step in identifying any raptor is estimating its overall size. Is it "large" like a Red-tailed Hawk (22 inches long) or "small" like an American Kestrel (10 inches)? Next, take note of obvious colors and patterns, such as facial markings, "belly-bands," and whether the underparts are barred (horizontally) or streaked (vertically).

Range and Season
Frequently you can make an identification by a process of elimination. Once you have narrowed down the possibilities by observing size and field marks, consider the bird's range and the season in which you are observing it. A buteo on the western plains in winter is not likely to be a Swainson's Hawk, because their wintering grounds are in Argentina.

13

Similarly, a boldly patterned bird seen on the Atlantic coast in summer is no doubt an Osprey rather than the often similarly patterned Rough-legged Hawk, because all Rough-legs are on their Arctic breeding grounds in summer.

Habitat Considering the type of habitat in which a bird is sighted can help in identification as well. Accipiters, with their short wings and long tails, are adapted for maneuverability in dense forests and thickets. They are usually seen in open country only during migration, when their favored forests may not be close at hand. Falcons, however, with their long, pointed wings, are high-speed birds of open plains, fields, and marshes. So a raptor seen hunting in the forest is not likely to be a falcon. Buteos, the large, wide-winged, soaring hawks of open country, are most often seen slowly circling over farmlands, prairies, and marshes.

Flight Because birds of prey are often seen only in flight, or at a considerable distance, standard field marks are often muted by sunlight, shade, or distance. Soaring hawks often appear as silhouettes against the sky. The observer must concentrate on what some birdwatchers refer to as the "jizz," or gestalt, of a bird—some overall look or impression that may be difficult to analyze but somehow suggests the given species. In such situations, a whole new group of identification techniques is used, methods that assess shape, flight pattern, movement, and behavior. To help you acquire these skills, a special section of this guide deals specifically with raptors in flight, detailing specific or likely traits to look for.

A Helpful Tip   In looking at field marks, don't let the common names of birds confuse you. While many Red-tailed Hawks do show bright, brick-red tails, other species have reddish tails as well, and young Red-tails have brown, banded tails. Broad-winged Hawks do not have particularly broad wings; and probably only bird-banders and museum curators have ever seen the sharp keel on the legs of a Sharp-shinned Hawk.

Watching Birds of Prey

There are numerous places to observe birds of prey throughout North America. While some birds of prey are generally found in remote, wild areas, many species are commonly encountered in and around towns, suburban areas, and along roadsides. This is particularly true during migration periods, in both spring and fall, when birds may be found far from their usual haunts.

Time of Day Because owls are mainly nocturnal predators, only the observer out at dawn or dusk is likely to see them. Hawks, eagles, and vultures, however, are daytime flyers, most likely to be seen flying between about 9:00 a.m. and 2:00 p.m. on sunny days. During that period, rising bodies of warm air, called thermals, assist their soaring flight.

Locations Most raptors require large territories through which to move and hunt, so vast, unfragmented forests and farmlands are usually the best places to find them. National parks, state parks, and any large tracts of public land are prime places to search. Many hawks, including Red-tailed Hawks and American Kestrels, are often seen along grassy roadsides, where rodents and insects can be abundant. Driving along back roads that carry little traffic is an excellent way to spot them. Because hawks are usually very

16

wary, your car often works as a blind, or "hide," and provides a good vantage point for both observation and photography. A spotting scope, a birdwatcher's telescope mounted on a sturdy tripod, can be a useful—even necessary—tool because of the great distances at which hawks are usually seen. It will often provide much better views than binoculars.

Migration The best time to watch hawks is during migratory periods in spring and fall. In both the summer and winter, the secretive nature of some species and the large territories of others often do not offer many viewing opportunities. During migration, however, birds of prey are concentrated by habitat, wind direction, and particularly geography. Often, concentrations are of such magnitude that an observer can see more hawks in a few hours than he or she might see in many years of watching in breeding areas or on wintering grounds. Such concentrations usually occur along mountain ridges, where migrating raptors gain lift and an easy ride on winds deflected upward over the peaks, or along the coasts, where geography concentrates birds of prey reluctant to fly out over water.

17

The Birds

Black Vulture *Coragyps atratus*

John J. Audubon, who called this species the Carrion Crow, reported that it was a common sight in many southern cities, including Charleston and Savannah, hopping about the streets and perching on the roofs. It was Audubon, in fact, who began a famous debate over whether vultures find their food by sight or by smell; researchers have since determined that this species relies largely on vision. Black Vultures are known to associate in small family groups.

Identification 22–24". A large black bird often seen soaring in groups with Turkey Vultures. There are conspicuous white patches on the outer third of the wings. The Black Vulture flaps its wings more often and more rapidly than does the Turkey Vulture, and its tail is much shorter.

Voice Seldom vocal; occasionally hisses or utters guttural noises.

Habitat Often soars above open land, including agricultural areas, pastures, and roadsides; roosts in open woodlands.

Range Primarily the southeastern U.S., ranging to the midwestern states; range has been expanding northward, rarely as far north as Maine.

Turkey Vulture *Cathartes aura*

This most common species of vulture is a distant relative of Merriam's Condor, a now-extinct Ice Age scavenger with a 12-foot wingspan. Less than one-quarter the size of its ancient relative, but sizable as compared with present-day birds, the Turkey Vulture spends much of its time ridding the landscape of garbage and carrion. This species apparently uses its keen sense of smell to locate food.

Identification 25–32". A large black bird showing contrasting light hind-wing and dark fore-wing feathers as seen from below. In flight, it carries its wings in a shallow-V shape. Close up, the red, featherless head is apparent in adult birds.

Voice Normally silent; occasionally hisses or utters guttural noises.

Habitat Often soars above open land, including agricultural areas, pastures, and roadsides; roosts in deciduous woodlands.

Range Across most of the U.S., expanding into northern New England, where it was once rare; winters north to California and southern New England.

California Condor *Gymnogyps californianus*

Accounts from the mid-19th century indicate that this species was scarce even then. Throughout most of the 20th century the California Condor was harassed, shot, and even poisoned, and by the 1970s scarcely 30 birds survived. During the 1980s researchers captured the few remaining wild birds and began captive breeding programs. These have been successful, but it remains to be seen if reintroduction into natural habitats will ultimately succeed.

Identification 45–55". A massive black bird with wingspan up to 9'. Adults show large areas of white feathers on the forward part of the wing. They have reddish-orange, featherless heads and black ruffs or neck collars.

Voice Normally silent.

Habitat Mountainsides and open brush country. Nests on cliffside ledges.

Range Historically, from the Columbia River in Oregon south through Lower California. During the 20th century, restricted to southern California.

Osprey *Pandion haliaetus*

Ospreys subsist entirely on fish. These "fish hawks" sight fish while hovering above the water, then dive and grasp the prey with their talons. North American Osprey populations were devastated by the use of DDT during the 1950s and 1960s. Fortunately, however, by the mid-1970s DDT was largely banned. Encouraged by artificial nesting platforms, Ospreys began to make a comeback.

Identification 21–24". A large brown (the brown often appears black) and white bird. Seen from below, the Osprey shows long, crooked wings with dark "wrist" patches. There is a dark, masklike line on the side of its face, running through the eye.

Voice A loud, repeated whistle.

Habitat Wetland habitats, especially coastal marshes, as well as lakes and rivers.

Range Breeds from Alaska and Newfoundland south along both coasts; occasionally inland near lakes and rivers. Winters in southernmost states and southward.

Hook-billed Kite *Chondrohierax uncinatus*

Primarily a resident of the tropics, this species is rare in North America. Hawk aficionados seeking the Hook-billed Kite in the United States must travel to the lower Rio Grande Valley in southern Texas. There, at places such as Falcon Dam, Bentsen–Rio Grande State Park, and Santa Ana National Wildlife Refuge, a few pairs of Hook-billed Kites are residents. Like the Snail Kite of southern Florida, this species feeds on snails.

Identification 15–17". Perhaps the most distinctive feature of this hawk is the shape of its wings. They are paddlelike: relatively narrow at the base and broader toward the tip. The bird also has a long, banded tail. Males are generally gray and are heavily barred below; females are rusty brown. At close range the characteristic large, hooked bill is apparent.

Voice A musical whistle; also a rattle during courtship.

Habitat Mesquite woodlands bordering rivers and streams.

Range In the U.S., restricted to southernmost Texas.

American Swallow-tailed Kite *Elanoides forficatus*

This spectacular raptor flies with particular agility and grace. Sociable by nature, it is often seen hunting in small groups, swooping and gliding in and out of open woodlands in seemingly effortless maneuvers. Perhaps its ability as an aerialist accounts for the fact that it spends much of its time in the air, seldom going to perch. The American Swallow-tailed Kite even feeds in the air, taking a variety of insects, lizards, and snakes. When thirsty it also stays on the wing, drinking as it skims the surface of a pond or stream.

Identification 22–24". An unmistakable black and white bird with pointed wings and a deeply forked, swallowlike tail.

Voice A shrill, whistled *klee klee klee.*

Habitat Open southern woodlands and adjacent wetlands, including river bottoms.

Range Texas, east along the Gulf Coast through Florida, and north to South Carolina. Winters south of the U.S.

White-tailed Kite *Elanus leucurus*

Typically, raptors and other birds are adversely affected by invasive human activity. The White-tailed Kite seems to be an exception to the rule. During the 1930s and 1940s this species became rare on its southern California breeding grounds. Subsequently, agricultural activity increased in that area, and the kite's numbers grew. A healthy mouse population may have been largely responsible, and it continues to provide the White-tailed Kite with an abundance of its favorite prey. This bird was previously called the Black-shouldered Kite.

Identification	16". A basically white and gray bird, showing a white tail and black "wrist" patches as seen from below. When perched, its black shoulders and red eyes are visible.
Voice	A series of chirps; also a descending whistle.
Habitat	Open grasslands, fields, and agricultural areas.
Range	Coastal California, Arizona, and the Gulf Coast; rare but breeding in southern Florida.

Snail Kite *Rostrhamus sociabilis*

The Snail Kite is one of numerous species in southern Florida that have suffered because of the ever-growing needs of the human population. It feeds almost exclusively on apple snails, whose populations are being drastically reduced as wetlands are drained and channelized for development and agricultural purposes. Fewer than two dozen birds survived in Florida in the mid-1960s. Last-minute conservation efforts seem to have been effective, however, as counts of more than 700 birds were made during the 1980s.

Identification 16–18". A handsome raptor; adult males are overall slate-black with bright red legs. In flight birds show a characteristic tail pattern: a broad white area at the base, a wide black band in the middle, and a narrow buff terminal band. (See also page 36.)

Voice A repetitious cackle when disturbed, as well as a harsh greeting call.

Habitat Freshwater wetlands.

Range In the U.S., restricted to southern Florida.

34

Snail Kite *Rostrhamus sociabilis*
Female (see also page 34)

Identification 16–18". Adult female and immature Snail Kites are brown above and darkly streaked below, with a white throat and forehead patch. Adult females have bright orange legs. In flight they show a characteristic tail pattern: broadly white at the base, with a wide black band in the center and a narrow buff terminal band.

Nesting Snail Kites may nest alone or in small groups of 6 or more pairs. Their loosely constructed, stick nest may be on the ground, in a bush, or in a tree to 15' above the water. Two to five brown-blotched, white eggs are laid and incubated by both adults. Young Snail Kites are capable of flight approximately 1 month after hatching.

Mississippi Kite *Ictinia mississippiensis*

The Mississippi Kite is a marvelous flier, spending hour upon hour aloft. John J. Audubon noted that its aerial skills could be compared only to those of the Swallow-tailed Kite. Interestingly, it seldom circles in the typical soaring pattern of other raptors, but rather moves along in a more or less straight line, sometimes veering to one side. Like several of its kin, the Mississippi Kite even feeds while airborne.

Identification
: 12–14". A relatively small bird, looking much like a falcon with long, narrow wings. It flies in a buoyant, casual manner. On the wing, adults are overall gray with light heads and dark tails. In flight the tail often appears square-tipped or notched. (See also page 40.)

Voice
: A high, thin whistle, repeated once or twice.

Habitat
: Open grasslands and bottomlands with suitable perches and nesting trees.

Range
: Mainly the southern U.S., from Arizona and the southern plains to the Gulf Coast, Florida panhandle, and South Carolina. Winters south of the U.S.

Mississippi Kite *Ictinia mississippiensis*
Immature (see also page 38)

Identification 12–14". In general, the Mississippi Kite looks like a small
falcon with long, narrow wings. Seen in flight from below,
immatures show the typical gray flight feathers but also a
good deal of brown in the wing coverts. The body is heavily
streaked below in the youngest birds and grayish splotched
with white in subadults. In flight the tail often appears
square-tipped and notched. These birds fly in a buoyant,
casual manner.

Nesting Although several pairs of Mississippi Kites may associate
during the nesting season, they normally nest in separate
locations. Their stick nest is placed in a tree between 12' and
80' above the ground. One to three bluish-tinged, white eggs
are laid and incubated by both adults. Young Mississippi
Kites leave the nest a little over 1 month after hatching.

Bald Eagle *Haliaeetus leucocephalus*

Bald Eagles have a varied diet, but fish constitute a majority of their food. Their fish-eating habits, like those of the Osprey, have resulted in drastic population declines, especially during the era of widespread DDT use. Less than two centuries after it was chosen as our national emblem, this species was listed as either threatened or endangered in all states except Alaska. A reduction in the use of lethal pesticides, and active recovery programs, however, have helped to reverse this trend. In fact, Bald Eagles are once again successfully nesting over much of their former range.

Identification
31–32". Adults are nearly unmistakable, given their large size, dark bodies, and snow-white heads and tails. Young birds are variously marked with white (see also page 44).

Voice
Harsh, metallic cackles.

Habitat
Almost invariably adjacent to wetlands, especially along coastlines and around large lakes and rivers.

Range
Widespread in Alaska; more restricted in the contiguous 48 states, but found regularly along the Pacific and Atlantic coasts, in the Northwest, and in Florida.

Bald Eagle *Haliaeetus leucocephalus*
Immature (see also page 42)

Identification 31–32". Young Bald Eagles take 3–4 years to acquire adult plumage and are variously marked with white feathers, depending on their age. In their first year, birds typically have largely dark bodies, tails, and head feathers. Second- and third-year birds are called "white-bellies" because of the white streaking on their stomachs, underwings, and backs. Subadult birds have heads and tails that are largely white but are streaked with dark feathers.

Nesting Bald Eagles build massive stick nests that may be 8' across and up to 12' deep. The nest may be placed on the ground or on a rocky cliff face. More commonly it is constructed high in a tree. Normally 2 eggs are laid, although only 1 chick will survive if food is not plentiful. Young eagles are capable of flight approximately 10 weeks after hatching.

White-tailed Eagle *Haliaeetus albicilla*

The White-tailed Eagle, once called the White-tailed Sea Eagle, is a fish eater. Like the Bald Eagle, these birds are known for their thievery, although they do capture fish themselves. At times the White-tailed Eagle will let another bird, such as a gull, actually catch the prey and then proceed to harry the bird until it drops the fish. The White-tailed Eagle also takes advantage of annual salmon runs, when a ready supply of dying fish is available.

Identification 33". Similar to the Bald Eagle but lacking the white head; however, the brown head feathers are relatively pale, so the head sometimes has a white appearance. The cream-colored tail is stubby and wedge-shaped; undertail coverts are dark. Young birds are variously marked with white, as is found with Bald Eagles.

Voice Harsh, metallic cackles, similar to the Bald Eagle's.

Habitat Coastal areas with a ready supply of fish.

Range An Old World species. In North America, restricted to the Aleutian Islands (also recorded from Kodiak Island). Breeds in Greenland and the eastern Canadian Arctic.

46

Steller's Sea Eagle *Haliaeetus pelagicus*

Like the White-tailed Eagle, this species is primarily
a resident of eastern Asia. Recently, however, a Steller's
Sea Eagle has been a regular resident at Taku Inlet near
Juneau, Alaska. The species was named for Georg Wilhelm
Steller, a naturalist who, along with Vitus Bering, was
among the first Europeans to explore and describe the
animals in this part of the New World. Steller's Eider
(*Polysticta stelleri*), a small eider of Alaska and the
Aleutians, also bears his name.

Identification 27–37". Similar to the Bald Eagle in overall appearance but
almost a third again as large, with wingspan to 8'. It has a
massive bill, white shoulders (in flight, the leading edge of
the wing), and a white, wedge-shaped tail.

Voice A barklike *kra-kra-kra.*

Habitat Coastal islands and inlets where a ready supply of fish and
birds is available.

Range A Siberian species. In North America, restricted to the
Aleutians, Pribilofs, and Kodiak Island.

Northern Harrier *Circus cyaneus*

Formerly called Marsh Hawk, this species is the only North American representative of the harrier group. These birds are noted for their unusual hunting behavior. They fly only a few feet off the ground over open country and marshes, ever ready to pounce on small rodents, various reptiles, and occasionally even birds. A characteristic facial disk enables the hawk to locate its prey through sound.

Identification 16–24". A slim, long-winged, long-tailed raptor whose most obvious field mark is a conspicuous white rump. Its back-and-forth, low-to-the-ground, slightly rocking flight is also a good clue to identification. At close range, the owl-like face can be discerned. Adult males are gray overall. Females and immature birds are mainly brown (see also pages 52 and 54).

Voice Normally silent; at times utters a shrill *kee kee kee*.

Habitat Coastal and inland marshes, as well as open meadows, fields, and grasslands.

Range Breeds from Alaska east to the eastern seaboard, south through the central U.S. Winters across most of the southern U.S.

50

Northern Harrier *Circus cyaneus*
Female (see also pages 50 and 54)

Identification   16–24". Because of their greater numbers in overall
Northern Harrier populations, females and immatures are
more often observed than are the gray adult males. They
are slim, long-winged, long-tailed raptors. Their most
obvious field mark is a conspicuous white rump. Females are
largely brown above. They show a tawny belly, heavily
streaked with darker feathers. The birds' back-and-forth,
low-to-the-ground, slightly rocking flight is also a good clue
to identification. Close up, the owl-like face is apparent.

Nesting   Northern Harrier females build a nest of sticks and grasses.
It is normally placed on a low bush or among the reeds in
or near a marsh. Normally 5 light blue eggs are laid and
incubated by the female. Young Northern Harriers are
capable of flight approximately 1 month after hatching.

Northern Harrier *Circus cyaneus*
Immature (see also pages 50 and 52)

Identification 16–24". Immature and female Northern Harriers are more likely to be observed than males because there are more of them. Immature birds are mostly brown above, rust- or cream-colored below, and appear streaked. The white rump; long, narrow wings; and low, rocking flight are the best clues to identification. The characteristic owl-like face may be seen at close range.

Sharp-shinned Hawk *Accipiter striatus*

Smallest of the three accipiters in North America, the Sharp-shinned Hawk specializes in chasing down small songbirds in deep woodlands. While these hawks appear to be holding their own in the West, several long-term studies in the East point to a dramatic decrease in their numbers. An apparent decline in several species of songbirds on which the hawk relies may be the cause of this development.

Identification 10–14". A small, jay-sized accipiter with short, rounded wings and a long tail. Very similar to Cooper's Hawk (see page 58) but with a relatively small head and eyes, a squared-off tail, and a more buoyant flight, characteristically consisting of quick flaps interspersed with glides.

Voice Normally silent; occasionally utters a sharp *kick kick kick.*

Habitat Northern boreal forest and deciduous woodlands. In winter, may stalk smaller birds around feeding stations.

Range Breeds from Alaska east to Newfoundland and south along the Appalachians and in western mountain states. Winters throughout the U.S.

Cooper's Hawk *Accipiter cooperii*

During the 1950s and 1960s, when many of the songbirds and other prey of Cooper's Hawks were ingesting DDT and similar pesticides, the reproductive success of this raptor was poor. An apparent reversal of this trend over the succeeding two decades strengthened the Cooper's Hawk's numbers. This accipiter is most common in the West, where it is found nesting regularly in streamside woodlands or open forests.

Identification	14–20". The medium-sized accipiter of North America, this crow-sized raptor has noticeably short, rounded wings and a long tail. As compared with the Sharp-shinned Hawk (see page 56), the Cooper's Hawk has a larger head and flies with a more deliberate wing beat. Its tail appears rounded at the tip; when perched it shows raised hackles.
Voice	Alarm call is a loud *cack cack cack*.
Habitat	Open, deciduous or mixed woodlands.
Range	Breeds throughout southern Canada and most of the U.S., except the central plains and southern Florida. Winters across most of the U.S.

Northern Goshawk *Accipiter gentilis*

The ability of this large accipiter to maneuver through
dense woodlands is spectacular. Primarily a resident of
northern coniferous forests, the Northern Goshawk uses
its agility to prey on other forest-dwelling birds. It is known
for its tenacious territorial defense; hikers who wander
unknowingly into the goshawk's nesting area will be
"greeted" by raucous calls. If the intruders do not retreat,
the accipiter will press the attack, swooping like a shadow in
and out of the trees. It may even strike the trespassers with
its powerful talons.

Identification	20–26". A large bird; the female is as large as a Red-tailed Hawk. Adult birds are largely gray with fine gray barring below; young birds are brown with heavy streaking below. There is a bold white line above the eye.
Voice	A loud *keek keek keek keek;* also a slurred *keeah.*
Habitat	Mainly coniferous forests; at times mixed woodlands.
Range	Alaska east to Newfoundland, forested mountains in the western U.S. east to New England, and as far south as the Appalachians.

Common Black Hawk *Buteogallus anthracinus*

A tropical species, the Common Black Hawk is actually a rarity in the United States. Even the small population that does occur in the Southwest seems to be declining. This bird tends to prefer aquatic prey. Sometimes it swoops down quietly from a low perch toward a pond or stream, from which it takes a variety of frogs and fish. At other times it walks along streambanks and mud flats in search of crayfish and crabs.

Identification	20–23". The adult is overall black, with broad black wings and a short, stubby tail with a broad white band across the middle. Immature birds are brown above and heavily streaked below.
Voice	A long, harsh *ka-a-a-ah;* also a high-pitched whistle.
Habitat	A variety of open, woodland situations, including canyons and streamside bottomlands.
Range	Utah south to southern Arizona, southwestern New Mexico, and southwestern Texas. Winters south of the U.S.

Harris' Hawk *Parabuteo unicinctus*

Harris' Hawk is a strikingly attractive raptor. Once called Bay-winged Hawk, it has distinctive chestnut, black, and white feathers that make it a favorite among falconers. Its hunting behavior is also of interest. Harris' Hawks often engage in cooperative hunting, in which two or three birds work together to capture rabbits, ground squirrels, and gophers. Cooperation among Harris' Hawks also extends to their nesting activities, in which up to five family members may be associated with one nest site. A typical group may comprise two adult males and one adult female, with one or two immature birds to help with chick-rearing.

Identification 17½–29". Adults are overall dark brown with bright chestnut shoulders and thighs. The tail pattern consists of a broad white band at the base, a broad black band in the middle, and a narrow white terminal band.

Voice Loud, harsh screams.

Habitat Dry, scrub and brush country of the Southwest.

Range Southern Arizona, southeastern New Mexico, and southeastern Texas.

Gray Hawk *Buteo nitidus*

Basically a tropical species, the Gray Hawk is restricted to a handful of areas in the Southwest. It nests among streamside sycamores and cottonwoods in such picturesque spots as Sonoita Creek in Patagonia, Arizona. Befitting its woodland habitat, this buteo is somewhat accipiter-like, with a longish tail and rounded wings. The Gray Hawk uses its maneuverability to capture a variety of lizards, snakes, and frogs.

Identification 16–18". The adult is pearl-gray above with fine gray-and-white barring below and a black-and-white banded tail. Young birds are brown above and white streaked with brown below.

Voice A plaintive, downslurred whistle.

Habitat Streamside woodlands.

Range Mainly southern Arizona; a few in extreme southern Texas.

Roadside Hawk *Buteo magnirostris*

While widely distributed in the New World tropics, this hawk was unheard of in the United States until the mid-1980s. During the winter of 1982–83, a single Roadside Hawk spent the season in and around Bentsen–Rio Grande State Park, in the lower Rio Grande Valley of southern Texas. It is still considered accidental in the United States, but occasional reports of Roadside Hawk sightings continue to be made by birdwatchers visiting this favorite birding region. As their name implies, these hawks often may be seen along roadsides; they regularly perch on telephone poles and wires.

Identification 13–14". Similar to the Broad-winged Hawk, in that it is brown above with reddish barring below, but there is a distinctive dark bib on the upper chest. The bib on young birds is streaked brown and white.

Voice A shrill scream.

Habitat Uses a variety of open and semiopen wooded habitats.

Range Lower Rio Grande Valley in Texas.

Red-shouldered Hawk *Buteo lineatus*

Owls and hawks provide good examples of what biologists call "replacement" species. At night, owls replace hawks as active predators over much of the same habitat. In the lower, wooded wetlands, the Barred Owl replaces the Red-shouldered Hawk. During the day, the Red-shouldered Hawk actively seeks snakes, frogs, and the like.

Identification 16–24". Adults have reddish shoulders and barred under-parts. In flight, this hawk shows a pale crescent on the outer portion of the wing toward the tip. There are reddish to rust feathers on the forward part of wings, and a black-and-white banded tail. A variety of "light" to "dark" forms vary geographically. (See also page 72.)

Voice A strident series of downslurred shrieks: *ke-er, ke-er, ke-er, ke-er!*

Habitat A variety of wetlands, including maple swamps, southern cypress swamps, and streamside woodlands.

Range From the Great Lakes region east to New Brunswick, and south to eastern Texas; also California.

70

Red-shouldered Hawk *Buteo lineatus*
Immature (see also page 70)

Identification 16–24". In immature Red-shouldered Hawks the shoulder patch is brown rather than reddish, the body below is streaked with brown, and the tail pattern is less distinct than in adults, being dark brown with light tan bands.

Nesting The Red-shouldered Hawk's nest consists of sticks, bark, and mosses and often includes fresh evergreen cuttings. It is placed in a deciduous or coniferous tree 20–60' above the ground. Typically 2 brown-blotched, white eggs are laid and incubated by both adults. Young Red-shouldereds leave the nest approximately 5 weeks after hatching.

Broad-winged Hawk *Buteo platypterus*

During September in the eastern United States, the annual movement south of Broad-winged Hawks occurs. On mountaintops from Maine to Georgia, hawkwatchers gather to witness hundreds, thousands, rarely even tens of thousands of Broad-winged Hawks as they come together in spectacular flocks, called kettles, to travel to their wintering grounds in South America. Aided by thermals, created as warm air rises from the land, the hawks soar together in great circles, ever gaining altitude, and finally break off to sail swiftly southward in search of the next set of thermals.

Identification 13–15". Adults are brown above with reddish barring below. In flight, they show distinct, dark wing outlines, especially noticeable on the tips and trailing edges, and a black tail with a broad white band. (See also page 76.)

Voice A very high-pitched, thin whistle: *pee, peeeeee!*

Habitat Deciduous and mixed woodlands.

Range Throughout the eastern U.S. and southern Canada. Winters in southern Florida and the tropics.

Broad-winged Hawk *Buteo platypterus*
Immature (see also page 74)

Identification   13–15". The Broad-winged is one of the common buteos of
eastern North America, regularly seen in large numbers in
fall as they move southward. Immature Broad-winged
Hawks are brown above with light underparts variably
streaked with brown. The tail, broadly and distinctly
patterned in adults, shows less contrast in immature birds.
It displays indistinct, alternately light and dark bands.

Nesting   The Broad-winged Hawk's nest consists of sticks, lichens,
and fresh evergreen or oak cuttings. The nest is normally
placed 15–50' above the ground in a pine or oak tree.
Typically 2–3 eggs are laid and incubated by both adults.
Young birds are capable of flight approximately 6 weeks
after hatching.

Short-tailed Hawk *Buteo brachyurus*

This hawk is a tropical species, reaching the United States only in Florida. It is an inveterate bird hunter, which is rare in buteos, and is often seen kiting, or hanging in the wind, high overhead. When it spots likely prey, it makes spectacular dives, or "stoops," into the open forest. Like other, more common North American hawks, it occurs in two distinct color forms, or "morphs." Identification is complicated by the fact that the Short-tailed resembles the Broad-winged, Swainson's, Red-tailed, and Rough-legged hawks.

Identification 13–14". Similar in size and shape to the Broad-winged Hawk (see page 74); both morphs are dark above and show a black-and-white banded tail in flight. From below, the light form, shown here, has a white body and forward wing section. In the dark form, these areas are black.

Voice Screams or cackles when disturbed at nest.

Habitat Mixed woodlands and savanna; in winter, often near or around cypress and mangrove wetlands.

Range Southern Florida.

78

Swainson's Hawk *Buteo swainsoni*

The common western buteo of open country, Swainson's Hawk occurs in a variety of plumages, ranging from light to dark and including intermediate forms. Most winter on the pampas of Argentina; in March, they begin their long return journey to North American nesting territories. During April, large numbers of migrant Swainson's Hawks can be seen moving through Texas on their way to the plains and prairies of the United States and Canada.

Identification 18–22". This species' long, pointed wings are characteristic. Light morphs are mostly white below, with dark chestnut bibs and white throats. Dark flight feathers contrast with light underwing areas. This hawk soars with its wings held in a shallow-V shape. (See page 82 for dark phase.)

Voice A high-pitched, drawn-out scream: *kreeeer!*

Habitat Open plains and prairies with suitable perches and nesting trees.

Range A western bird. Breeds from Canada to Texas. Winters south of the U.S. and uncommonly in southern Florida.

80

Swainson's Hawk *Buteo swainsoni*
Dark Morph (see also page 80)

Identification 18–22". The long, pointed wings of this species are characteristic. Dark morphs show little or no contrast to the underwing; it is dark throughout. The body feathers are dark as well, but the undertail coverts (where the tail meets the body) are light. A variation on the dark-phase Swainson's Hawk has a dark brown bib and rufous body feathers.

Nesting The Swainson's Hawk's bulky stick and grass nest may be 4' in diameter and is often a refurbished structure used in successive years. Placement varies from on the ground to in low shrubs, trees, or even cactus. Normally 2 white eggs are laid and incubated by both parents. Young Swainson's Hawks leave the nest approximately 1 month after hatching.

White-tailed Hawk *Buteo albicaudatus*

Within the United States, this handsome buteo is restricted to the coastal prairies of southern Texas. A year-round resident there, it feeds on a variety of small mammals, reptiles, and insects. Like some other hawks, the White-tailed is an opportunist. When prairie fires race across the dry grasslands, many prey animals are forced from cover. The White-taileds, apparently attracted by the smoke, gather in groups around these fires to take advantage of the fleeing rabbits, cotton rats, and the like.

Identification 21–23". Adults are muddy gray above, and when perched they show a conspicuous rusty shoulder patch. Seen in flight from below, the body and forward portions of the wing are white; the white tail is especially short, with a single, broad black band.

Voice High-pitched screams: *kee-kee-kee-kee* or *cutta-cutta-cutta-cutta*.

Habitat Open grasslands and agricultural areas.

Range Extreme southern Texas.

Zone-tailed Hawk *Buteo albonotatus*

The Zone-tailed Hawk looks and acts like a Turkey Vulture. Its underwings are similarly patterned, and the hawk soars with wings held in a shallow-V shape typical of the vulture. The fact that Zone-tailed Hawks are often found flying with Turkey Vultures has led some researchers to conclude that a pattern of mimicry has evolved, allowing the hawk to approach its prey without eliciting the normal responses. This may also cause birdwatchers to dismiss a Zone-tailed Hawk as "just another vulture."

Identification 18½–21½". Slate-black above, with two-toned dark and light wings as seen from below. The black-and-white banded ("zoned") tail is a useful field mark. At close range, the raptor's yellow cere and feathered head distinguish it from all vultures.

Voice Loud, downslurred screams.

Habitat Wooded canyons, and streamside woodlands associated with scrub and desert country.

Range Arizona, southern New Mexico, and western Texas. Winters mainly south of the U.S.

86

Red-tailed Hawk *Buteo jamaicensis*

The Red-tailed Hawk is the most common buteo in North America. It is equally at home in mountains, deserts, prairies, and farmlands. A year-round resident in most of the United States, the Red-tailed is the hawk most likely to be seen along highways. Utility poles and fence posts have become the accustomed perch of these birds.

Identification 18–25". A sometimes bewildering variety of forms occur across the continent. A dark belly band is most prevalent in the East and often absent elsewhere. Contrasting dark "wrist" marks appear on the forward part of the wing, and the tail is red on its upper surface and pinkish as seen from below. (See pages 90 and 92 for dark-morph and immature birds.)

Voice A downslurred, drawn-out, single scream: *keeer!*

Habitat Various (see above), but requiring trees (deciduous or evergreen) or cacti for nesting, as well as other suitable perches from which to hunt. Absent from dense forest.

Range Widespread in North America from Alaska and Nova Scotia south.

Red-tailed Hawk *Buteo jamaicensis*
Dark Morph (see also pages 88 and 92)

Identification 18–25". Dark-morph Red-tailed Hawks are common in the West. Several distinct types have been described, although all are basically dark above. Below, these "dark-form" birds can be overall rufous to black. They sometimes have a contrasting dark brown belly band. Tails vary from white to rufous to black.

"Krider's Red-tail" is a pale, Great Plains subspecies, with a white head and distinct white patches on the outer upperwing.

"Harlan's Red-tail" is a dark form that breeds in the Northwest and winters throughout the Midwest. Generally sooty in color, it has a contrasting pale chest and a white tail with a black band at the tip.

Red-tailed Hawk *Buteo jamaicensis*
Immature (see also pages 88 and 90)

Identification 18–25". Immature Red-tailed Hawks have most of the same
field marks as the typical adult, except the reddish tail. The
upper parts are overall brownish, as are the contrasting
marks below. In flight, birds show a dark belly band and
dark bar and "wrist" marks on the forward edge of the
wing. The tail is muddy brown, finely marked with narrow
black bands.

Nesting The Red-tailed Hawk's stick nest is normally located in
deciduous or mixed woodlands and is placed in an oak or
pine between 15' and 70' above the ground. Typically 2 or 3
faintly marbled, white eggs are laid and incubated by the
female. Male Red-taileds remain in attendance, however,
and regularly bring food to the female as she is setting.
Young Red-taileds leave the nest 5–6 weeks after hatching.

Ferruginous Hawk *Buteo regalis*

The Ferruginous Hawk, the largest buteo in North America, lives in the wide-open spaces of the West. The flight strategies it uses to locate prey are numerous. While these hawks sometimes hunt from a perch, they also circle high above the plains. When they spot prey, they may hover briefly to get a better look and then swoop down rapidly, striking the prey with their talons. Also, pairs of Ferruginous Hawks have been observed hunting together, with one bird driving the prey toward the other.

Identification 22½–25". A large buteo with rusty back and shoulders above. There are two color morphs. Light birds are very pale below and show a distinct, dark V formed by the rusty leg feathers. There are white patches on the upperwing in both forms. (See page 96 for dark morph.)

Voice A downslurred, gull-like *kaaah*.

Habitat Short-grass prairies, arid scrub, and brushlands.

Range A western bird. Breeds from southern Alberta and Saskatchewan to northern Texas. Winters from southern breeding range southward.

Ferruginous Hawk *Buteo regalis*
Dark Morph (see also page 94)

Identification   22½–25". Like the typical Ferruginous Hawk, dark morphs
have rusty backs and shoulders above. Birds in flight show
contrasting wing colors seen from below: dark in front (on
coverts) and white behind (on flight feathers). There is also
a light mark resembling a comma outlined in gray on the
outer third of the wing. The tail is light colored, and there
are white patches on the upperwing.

Nesting   While Ferruginous Hawks will occasionally nest on the
ground or on a ledge, they prefer to make their nests in
trees. Because these hawks often use the same nest year
after year, adding to and enlarging the structure with each
season, a well-used nest can be quite spectacular. Nesting
materials include bones, dung, sagebrush, roots, and various
grasses. The hawk's success or failure during the nesting
season is apparently quite closely related to the size of local
jackrabbit populations.

Rough-legged Hawk *Buteo lagopus*

A summer resident of the high Arctic, the Rough-legged Hawk is one of the few diurnal raptors that occur in the contiguous 48 states primarily as winter residents. The breeding success of the Rough-legged Hawk is more or less controlled by the numbers of small rodents, such as lemmings, available during the nesting season. Low lemming numbers lead to "flight years" in which large numbers of these hawks move south seeking alternative food sources.

Identification 19–24". A large, long-winged buteo that occurs in light and dark morphs. From below, light morphs have a wide, dark band toward the end of their light tail. All ages show dark "wrist" patches. Males have dark, biblike markings, and some females and all immatures have a dark belly band. (See page 100 for dark morph.)

Voice A long, downslurred *keeer!;* also plaintive whistles.

Habitat Open areas, including farmlands, marshes, and grasslands.

Range Breeds in the Far North. Winters throughout most of the U.S., except in the Southeast.

Rough-legged Hawk *Buteo lagopus*
Dark Morph (see also page 98)

Identification   19–24". Like its light-morph counterpart, the dark form
of the Rough-legged Hawk has a wide, dark (dusky in
immatures) band toward the end of its light tail. Besides
dark body feathers, the underwing is characterized by
darker feathers on the forward part of the wing and lighter
or silvery feathers behind and at the tips of the flight
feathers. Some dark birds lack the white in the tail but are
still distinguishable from the similar Swainson's Hawk by
the silvery flight feathers below.

Nesting   The Rough-legged Hawk's nest may be located in a tree
or on a rocky ledge sheltered by an overhang. Nests
consist of twigs and plants, and the same structures are
used in succeeding years. From 2–7 white eggs with
brownish markings are laid and incubated by the female.
Young Rough-leggeds leave the nest approximately 6 weeks
after hatching.

Golden Eagle *Aquila chrysaetos*

The Golden Eagle, one of the most magnificent birds of prey, is surprisingly agile, especially considering its overall size and a wingspan exceeding seven feet. This raptor is capable of overtaking ducks in midair and chasing down rabbits. Unfortunately, many of these eagles have been shot or poisoned. Breeding pairs may stay together for many years, often returning to the same nesting site.

Identification   30–41". A large bird, overall dark brown with golden highlights on the crown and nape. Young birds are variously marked with white feathers; their finely banded tails generally appear all-dark under normal field conditions.

Voice   Generally not heard; occasionally mews or yelps.

Habitat   Mountainsides and canyons, as well as open grasslands and prairie. Eastern salt marshes in winter.

Range   Primarily western. Breeds from Alaska east to Newfoundland, and in most western states. Winters throughout much of North America except the Southeast; rarely in the Northeast.

Crested Caracara *Caracara plancus*

The Crested Caracara, the national bird of Mexico, is perhaps surprisingly a member of the falcon family. However, unlike most other North American falcons, which regularly chase down their prey on the wing, caracaras take a more "down to earth" approach to feeding. Carrion is a main staple in their diet, and like the vultures with which they are often found, these raptors are attracted to road kills. Crested Caracaras do also take live prey.

Identification	20–25". Overall slate-brown with a dark, crested cap; a featherless, red face; and white neck feathers. Birds in flight show a white upper chest and throat and white markings near the tip of the wing. The tail is white with a black tip.
Voice	Normally silent, but its common name is derived from a cackling cry sometimes given from a conspicuous perch.
Habitat	Open prairies, deserts, and farmlands.
Range	Central Florida, southeastern and extreme southern Texas, and southern Arizona.

104

American Kestrel *Falco sparverius*

Once known as the Sparrow Hawk, this smallest of North American falcons is seen regularly in populated areas. It often perches on utility wires and poles, and in agricultural areas it hovers above the ground in search of prey. In the spring and fall, large numbers of American Kestrels may be seen, particularly along the coasts, as they move to and from their more northerly breeding sites.

Identification 9–12". A small falcon with relatively long, pointed wings, often seen hovering. The back and tail are rufous; the facial pattern features two black stripes. The adult male has blue-gray wings and a rusty tail with a black tip; the female has brown wings and a brown-banded tail.

Voice A shrill *killy killy killy*.

Habitat Open areas, including farms, grasslands, deserts, and woodland edges.

Range Widespread across North America, except northern Alaska and northernmost Canada. Migratory in northern part of its range.

Merlin *Falco columbarius*

At the top of many hawkwatchers' lists of favorites, the Merlin is an attractive little speed demon. Colloquial names such as "bullet hawk" and "blue streak" bespeak the Merlin's ability to accelerate and turn in flight. They are on the move for much of the day, but late afternoon, when the falcons do most of their hunting, is the prime time during which to observe their aerial acrobatics.

Identification 10–14". A medium, jay-sized falcon with a largish head and long, pointed wings. In flight, the Merlin appears relatively dark overall. Both sexes are heavily streaked below. Adult males are slate-blue above; females are brown.

Voice A high-pitched, rapid *klee klee klee.*

Habitat Nests on the tundra and in open boreal woodlands; in winter and on migration, found in various open habitats.

Range Breeds east from Alaska throughout Canada and south to Nova Scotia; also Montana, and Wyoming. An uncommon winter resident along both U.S. coasts and in the southern U.S.

Aplomado Falcon *Falco femoralis*

The Aplomado Falcon is a bird of the open plains. Like the White-tailed Hawk (see page 84), it sometimes takes advantage of grass fires to prey on animals that are flushed by the flames. More typically, however, the Aplomado Falcon hunts from a perch by darting out in swift, bee-line flight. This falcon last nested in the United States in the 1950s. Loss of habitat is the most probable reason that it is only a rare visitor north of the Mexican border. It is currently being reintroduced in Texas.

Identification
15–18". A bird of typical falcon shape, with rather dark, long, pointed wings; a slate blue-gray back, and a dark band across the belly. The head pattern is distinctive, with two light, eyebrowlike lines extending to the back of the head.

Voice
A rapid, repeated cry: *gack gack gack gack;* also a shrill *eek, eek.*

Habitat
Open brush, grasslands, and desert.

Range
Formerly nested in the Southwest along the Mexican border. Now reported only occasionally in southwestern Texas, New Mexico, and Arizona.

Prairie Falcon *Falco mexicanus*

Large predators at the top of the food chain, including falcons and eagles, often suffer at the hands of humans even when they are not the intended victims. Ranchers often resort to spreading poison; hunters use lead shot; and farmers introduce pesticides into the environment. Prairie Falcons have been killed by cyanide and lead poisoning, and their reproductive success has been reduced because of the eggshell-thinning caused by pesticides.

Identification	17–20". A large bird, similar to the Peregrine Falcon but typically lighter in overall color and lacking the heavy mustache. In flight, it shows black armpit (underwing) markings, usually extending well down the wing.
Voice	A shrill *kree, kree, kree,* heard at the aerie.
Habitat	Open country; often badlands, prairies, or plains, with suitable bluffs or cliffs for nesting.
Range	A year-round resident in the West, from the Canadian plains south to northern Mexico. A partial migrant; regularly withdraws from its northernmost nesting areas.

112

Peregrine Falcon *Falco peregrinus*

Peregrine Falcons occur worldwide and have been kept for sport purposes at least since the Middle Ages. Peregrines are essentially bird hawks whose hunting technique relies on spectacular "stoops," in which they fold their wings and go into a dive that ends with a midair strike. This species was especially hard hit during the 1960s by the use of DDT. In the East, Peregrines were wiped out completely. Reintroduction programs are meeting with success, however.

Identification 15–21". A large falcon with long, pointed wings and a black mustache pattern on the face. Adults are gray above and light below; young birds are dark brown above and heavily streaked below.

Voice At nest, alarm call is a harsh *cack, cack, cack;* otherwise, normally silent.

Habitat Nesting sites include cliffs, skyscrapers, and bridges. On migration, birds follow coasts or major rivers.

Range From the Aleutians and northern Alaska east to Greenland; south through parts of the western U.S. and sparingly in the East to the mid-Atlantic.

114

Gyrfalcon *Falco rusticolus*

King of North American falcons, the large Gyrfalcon is a rare winter visitor from the high Arctic. It offers a typical example of how prey populations in many ways control their predators. In years when supplies of ptarmigan, the Gyrfalcon's main food, are low, this falcon may actually forgo nesting. It may also make a long journey southward, feeding mainly on waterfowl and grouse.

Identification 20–25". A large bird with a variety of color forms, from white to black; gray birds are the most common. The Gyrfalcon lacks the heavy mustache of the Peregrine Falcon but often has a similarly placed, narrow marking. Compared with other falcons this species has a heavier body, broader wings, and a longer tail. (See page 118 for white morph.)

Voice A loud, harsh *kak, kak, kak.*

Habitat In the Arctic on tundra with suitable cliff sites for nesting; southward at coastal and inland wetlands and prairies.

Range Breeds in the Arctic south to Alaska and northernmost Canada. An uncommon but regular winter resident along the northern border states and occasionally farther south.

116

Gyrfalcon *Falco rusticolus*
White Morph (see also page 116)

Identification 20–25". This largest of North American falcons has broad, long, pointed wings and a long tail. There are few distinguishing characteristics other than its overall shape and size. White-form birds may even lack the slight mustache line seen in other phases.

Nesting Gyrfalcons typically nest on a well-protected ledge on the face of a cliff. A simple scrape or abandoned raven's nest is often used. Three to eight red-speckled, white or buff eggs are laid and incubated by the female. Young Gyrfalcons are normally on the wing 7 weeks after hatching.

Barn Owl *Tyto alba*

The Barn Owl's heart-shaped facial disk and relatively small eyes differentiate this species and its family (Tytonidae) from the more typical North American owls. Despite its small eyes, this owl has excellent daytime and nocturnal vision. Researchers have determined that the Barn Owl's exceptional hearing also plays an important part in nightly food gathering. Barn Owls roost in such places as abandoned buildings, caves, or cedar groves. The fact that they often nest in barns explains their name.

Identification 14–20". Birds have a cinnamon wash on the upper breast and on the head and upper parts. Below, the feathers are mainly white with dark speckling. Typical also are the heart-shaped face, small dark eyes, and long legs.

Voice A raspy screech—*skraaah, skraaah*—and a series of clicking sounds.

Habitat Open country, including farms, grasslands, and deserts.

Range A year-round resident throughout most of the U.S.; less common northward. Partly migratory.

Flammulated Owl *Otus flammeolus*

The name of this owl comes from a Latin word meaning "flame-colored." No doubt it was adopted because of the reddish highlights on the faces and backs of some of these owls. But gray as well as reddish color morphs occur, so some Flammulated Owls have no flame-colored feathers. Interestingly, there tend to be more reddish birds in the southern part of this owl's range and more grayish birds to the north. Flammulated Owls spend most of their time in dense coniferous woodlands, where they hunt moths, beetles, and other insects. During the nesting season, they are sometimes found in small colonies.

Identification 6–7". A tiny, screech-owl–like species with dark eyes. Both reddish and gray forms occur.

Voice A series of evenly paced, single or paired hollow hoots on one pitch: *who, who, who, who, who, who.*

Habitat In coniferous woodlands during the nesting season; in a variety of habitats on migration.

Range Breeds from southern British Columbia, the U.S. Rockies, and Pacific states south to Mexico. Winters south of the U.S.

Eastern Screech-Owl *Otus asio*

Owls are mentioned frequently in folklore and superstition and have been associated traditionally with graveyards, mystery, and "the dark side" in general. The screech-owl, given its eerie voice and close association with human environs, may well be the owl most responsible for these characterizations. In fact, the reputation of this benign little creature has more to do with human imagination than it does with the actual life history of the owl. Eastern Screech-Owls spend most of the daylight hours roosting in hollow trees. At times they perch at the front of the cavity to take advantage of the sun's warming rays during a snooze.

Identification   8½". A small owl with ear tufts and yellow eyes. The bill is normally pale. Birds occur in reddish, gray, and brown plumages and are streaked and barred with dark markings below. (See also Western Screech-Owl, page 126.)

Voice   A descending, nasal whinny; also a whistled tremolo, held on one pitch.

Habitat   Wooded streamsides, orchards, and open woodlots.

Range   Year-round resident throughout the central and eastern U.S.

Western Screech-Owl *Otus kennicottii*

Until recently, this species was considered the same as the Eastern Screech-Owl. Screech-owls seen in the far western and eastern sections of the country usually can be identified by geographical location alone, although there is a Whiskered Screech-Owl in the extreme Southwest (see page 128). Differentiating the two screech-owls in the middle of the country, where their ranges overlap, is difficult and relies mainly on voice. The Western Screech-Owl, like its eastern counterpart, is one of the more common owls of its region. It regularly frequents human environs.

Identification 8½". A small owl with ear tufts and yellow eyes. Birds are overall gray; the bill is normally black, and the underparts are finely streaked with dark feathers. (See also Eastern Screech-Owl, page 124.)

Voice A series of accelerating, single toots on one pitch; also a short trill paired with a longer trill.

Habitat Open woodlands and orchards, deserts, and suburban areas.

Range Year-round resident in the western U.S. north to coastal British Columbia and south to Mexico.

Whiskered Screech-Owl *Otus trichopsis*

Vocalizations play an important part in the life of birds.
Along with visual displays, songs and calls are their primary
means of communication. For nocturnal birds, auditory
signals are critical. Owls give a variety of hoots, whistles,
and "screeches" to establish territory and to attract mates.
The calls of the Whiskered Screech-Owl turn out to be
important to owl-watchers as well. Because this species
looks almost exactly like the Western Screech-Owl, it is best
identified by its voice. The best time to hear these hoots is
during the breeding season.

Identification   6½–8". A small owl with ear tufts and yellow eyes. Birds
are slightly smaller than the Western Screech Owl and
somewhat more heavily streaked.

Voice   A series of *toots* sounding like Morse code; also a series of
rapid, evenly spaced hoots.

Habitat   Oak and mixed forest woodlands of mountain canyons.

Range   Southeastern Arizona and southwestern New Mexico south
through Mexico.

Great Horned Owl *Bubo virginianus*

The Great Horned is the common "big owl" of North America. The typical hooting of Great Horned Owls (both male and female) is often heard in early winter when the nesting cycle begins. Males and females share domestic duties and are regularly found incubating eggs in February, an extremely early start. Because of their size and strength, they are capable of capturing prey as large as domestic cats, porcupines, and even Canada Geese. Rabbits and squirrels, however, make up much of their diet. Great Horned Owls are aggressive in defense of their nests, especially once the owlets have hatched.

Identification 25". A large owl, overall gray-brown to tawny, with barring on the belly. Prominent ear tufts, yellow eyes, and a white throat patch distinguish this species.

Voice A rhythmic pattern of deep hoots. commonly rendered as *"Who's awake? Me too!"*

Habitat A relatively wide range of habitats, including mixed woodlands, wetlands, deserts, and urban parks.

Range Widespread throughout North America.

Snowy Owl *Nyctea scandiaca*

Primarily an Arctic species, the Snowy Owl often hunts during daylight hours. No doubt this behavior is dictated, at least in part, by the fact that during the nesting season in the Arctic the sun seldom sets. On its homeland tundra, the Snowy Owl subsists mainly on lemmings. When prey populations are low, large numbers of these owls push south to winter, often taking up temporary residence along the northernmost coasts of the contiguous 48 states. Here, too, they are often active during the day and may be observed flying across marshes or perched on rooftops.

Identification | 24". A large white owl that lacks ear tufts and has yellow eyes. Young birds and females are heavily marked with dark splotches.

Voice | On breeding grounds, a shrill whistle; also croaking.

Habitat | Arctic tundra; in winter, along coastal marshes or inland at extensive wetlands and grasslands.

Range | Breeds in Arctic and sub-Arctic regions. Usually winters farther south to the northern border states, occasionally as far south as northern Alabama and central California.

Northern Hawk Owl *Surnia ulula*

Present-day owl aficionados who have yet to see this species can take consolation from the fact that John J. Audubon was in the same boat. In the "Hawk Owl" description found in his monumental *Birds of America,* Audubon bemoaned the fact that this species was unknown to him and that he therefore had to rely on the accounts of others. The Northern Hawk Owl is a resident primarily of Alaska and Canada in North America and is found in the contiguous 48 states only in winter; even then it occurs only in small numbers and usually to the far north. Like many boreal species, however, once located it is often tame and relatively easy to approach.

Identification	14½–17½". A medium-sized, long-tailed owl, active during the day. It has yellow eyes and black feathers that frame the face. The underparts are heavily barred.
Voice	A rapid, whistled tremolo that seems to accelerate; also a sharp *pik pik pik,* described as hawklike.
Habitat	Open, boreal woodlands and wetlands.
Range	Alaska east to Newfoundland along the boreal forest zone.

Northern Pygmy-Owl *Glaucidium gnoma*

Most owls, as well as many hawks and eagles, have digestive systems that allow them to swallow the bones, fur, and other nondigestible materials in their prey. Typically, these materials come together in pellets that are regurgitated. The observant naturalist often finds these pellets on the forest floor in the vicinity of owl nests and roosts. The Northern Pygmy-Owl is unusual in that it forms no pellets. It seems to be a bit more discriminating in its eating habits, although it does have a fairly typical diet for its size, consisting of many mice and insects.

Identification 7–7½". A tiny owl that lacks ear tufts and has yellow eyes and a long, barred tail. There are two characteristic eyelike markings on the hind neck. Gray and reddish morphs occur.

Voice A series of evenly paced whistles on one pitch, like single notes from a songflute; also a short, clicking rattle.

Habitat Open woodlands, both coniferous and mixed deciduous, often in canyons.

Range Resident from British Columbia south throughout the western states through Mexico, and east to the prairies.

136

Ferruginous Pygmy-Owl *Glaucidium brasilianum*

This owl is very common in Mexico and Central and South America but uncommon in North America. Because it is so similar to its close relative the Northern Pygmy-Owl, it is best identified by its voice. It includes among its favorite prey lizards and scorpions. In southern Arizona it may be found nesting in saguaro cacti; in the lower Rio Grande Valley of Texas it favors thorn scrub. The Ferruginous Pygmy-Owl is said to be crepuscular in its hunting habits, preferring the low-light situations of dawn and dusk.

Identification 6½–7". A tiny owl, overall reddish to gray. It has yellow eyes and a long, barred tail and lacks ear tufts. It differs from the Northern Pygmy-Owl (see page 136) in having a rusty tail with dark barring.

Voice Fast-paced whistles repeated on one relatively high pitch: *poip, poip, poip, poip.*

Habitat Deserts, scrublands, and streamsides.

Range Resident in southern Arizona deserts and the woodlands of the Rio Grande Valley in Texas, south through Central and South America.

Elf Owl *Micrathene whitneyi*

The Elf Owl is the smallest owl species in North America and a favorite among birders. Resident Elf Owls at Madera Canyon in Arizona and Bentsen–Rio Grande State Park in Texas often attract a crowd. This diminutive owl makes use of old woodpecker holes in saguaro cacti in southeastern Arizona and in deciduous trees in southern Texas. There is a small population in southern California, but Elf Owl numbers are declining there, so biologists have begun a reintroduction program. Insects are the mainstay of the Elf Owl's diet.

Identification 5–6". Overall gray-brown; it is identified by its tiny size, yellow eyes, stubby tail, and lack of ear tufts. There is also a line of white spots on the shoulder.

Voice A long whinny, rising and falling in pitch, and various whistles, among them a puppylike *keu, keu, keu.*

Habitat Wooded canyons, deserts, and scrub country.

Range Southern Arizona, southwestern New Mexico, southern California, and the southernmost regions of Texas. Winters south of the U.S.

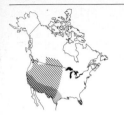

Burrowing Owl *Athene cunicularia*

The Burrowing Owl is a resident of open country, often forming colonies in prairie-dog towns. It perches on a prairie-dog mound on its especially long legs and issues a complex series of alarms to warn others of nearby predators. Nineteenth-century accounts of these western "towns" describe vast colonies. Since then, ranchers' programs to control prairie dogs have eliminated many of these areas and the Burrowing Owls along with them. The owls may still be found, however, in many of the remaining prairie-dog towns as well as at golf courses and airports.

Identification 9–11". Overall brown above with white spotting; white below with tan barring. It has long legs and a short tail.

Voice A dovelike *co-coo, co-coo;* also a bubbling *quick, quick, quick, quick.* When disturbed at its nest, it will hiss like a rattlesnake.

Habitat Prairies, open agricultural and disturbed areas, golf courses, airports, and even vacant lots in suburban neighborhoods.

Range Throughout the West; also southern Florida.

142

Spotted Owl *Strix occidentalis*

The Spotted may not be the biggest or the most spectacular owl in North America, but it is surely the most controversial one. After a long debate, the Spotted Owl was placed on the Endangered Species List in 1991. In its simplest terms, the political infighting pitted loss of logging jobs against the shrinking habitat of the endangered owl. The argument took on national import during the 1992 United States presidential election. The Spotted Owl now awaits its fate, surrounded by clear cuts in its native, old-growth forest.

Identification	16½–19". A medium-sized owl with brown eyes and a tuftless head. It is overall brown with white spotting.
Voice	A series of deep hoots, usually in pairs and well paced, similar to a dog barking: *who, who who, whoooo.* Also a slurred cry: *oohoohwee!*
Habitat	Temperate rain forest, wooded canyons, and mountainsides. Requires extensive, old-growth forest.
Range	Resident along the Pacific Coast, south along the Sierra Nevada; also the southern Rocky Mountains, Arizona, and New Mexico.

144

Barred Owl *Strix varia*

The Barred Owl is a fairly common resident of eastern North America. It is regularly found in the cypress swamps of the Southeast, where it often shares the habitat of the Red-shouldered Hawk. During the day it typically roosts quietly on its favorite perch and may often be approached quite closely. At dusk it begins its nighttime hunt and will prey on a wide variety of rodents, reptiles, amphibians, and occasionally small birds. The Barred Owl also fishes. It has been observed on the banks of creeks, creeping along cypress knees, and snatching fish from the water.

Identification 20". A medium-sized owl, brown overall, with dark brown eyes; barring on the upper chest, and streaking below.

Voice Often located by its vocalization. Typical call is a series of hoots, commonly represented as *"Who cooks for you, who cooks for you all?"*

Habitat Wetlands and their associated woodland cover. Lowlands in the South and wooded valleys and ridges in the North.

Range Widespread east of the Rockies, and expanding west through Canada to the Pacific Northwest.

146

Great Gray Owl *Strix nebulosa*

The Great Gray Owl is another species that usually occurs only as an irregular winter visitor to the contiguous 48 states. This "gray ghost" is our largest owl, but since much of its size can be attributed to feathers, it is easily outweighed by most Great Horned Owls. During sporadic flight years, greater than normal numbers of these owls make their way south in winter to the northern tier of the border states. Once a Great Gray Owl is located, it is easy to observe because these owls are characteristically tame, lacking experiences that might cause them to fear people.

Identification 24–33". A large owl, overall dusky gray with yellow eyes. There are dark concentric rings on the large facial disk and a white bow-tie mark at the "chin."

Voice A steady series of deep, mellow, haunting hoots: *who, who, who, who, wooh.*

Habitat Boreal forest and edges of coniferous forest.

Range A resident of the Far North, south to central California along the Sierra Nevada, and the northern Rockies. Occasionally winters south and east of normal range.

148

Long-eared Owl *Asio otus*

The so-called ears or horns of owls have little or nothing to do with hearing, but owls are quite well endowed with hearing equipment. They have large ear openings on the sides of the head, which are normally covered by feathers. Many species, including the nocturnal Long-eared Owl, have especially keen hearing and are often able to locate prey precisely by sound alone.

Identification 13–16". A medium-sized owl with long ear tufts placed relatively close together on the top of the head. There is a rusty facial disk. This owl is similar to the Great Horned Owl (see page 130) but smaller, with dark, vertical streaking rather than horizontal barring on the underparts.

Voice Likely to be heard only during breeding season. Sonorous hoots: *hooo hooo.* Also wails and whines.

Habitat Roosts colonially and nests in dense coniferous woodlands; hunts at night over open country.

Range Breeds from Canada south to California and Virginia. Migratory. Winters throughout the U.S., except for southern Florida.

Short-eared Owl *Asio flammeus*

The Short-eared Owl is a species of open country. While it occasionally roosts in woodlands, more often than not it spends the day under cover of marsh or prairie grasses. This owl even nests on the ground and is frequently found in small colonies. Because the Short-eared Owl does much of its hunting at dawn and dusk in open-country situations, it is relatively easy to find and observe. It hunts in a manner similar to that of the Northern Harrier, often coursing back and forth over a field, close to the ground. It hovers briefly, then drops down to snatch a vole or a mouse.

Identification 13–17". A medium-sized owl with dark eye patches. It is best identified in flight by its behavior (see above) and by black "wrist" patches on the lower surface of the wings and a buff patch above.

Voice A raspy, barked: *yip! yip! yip!*

Habitat Open fields, prairies, meadows, and salt marshes.

Range Widespread across North America; breeds from the Far North south through the central U.S. Migratory. Winters throughout the U.S.

152

Boreal Owl *Aegolius funereus*

Some birds have reputations among birdwatchers for their rarity. The Boreal Owl is such a species, occurring only rarely in or near the normal haunts of most birdwatchers. One of its few nesting locales in the contiguous 48 states is Cameron Pass in Colorado. There, high in the Rocky Mountains among the snowfields, rocky balds, and groves of alpine conifers, a few pairs of Boreal Owls annually raise their young. It is there also that more than a few birdwatchers have gone to add this Owl to their life lists.

Identification	8½–12". A small owl without ear tufts; heavily streaked with chocolate-brown feathers below. A black border is created by the feathers framing the facial disk, and there is a pale bill.
Voice	A rapid series of high-pitched, whistled hoots. In courtship, a series of notes compared to that of a soft bell, rising and falling in pitch.
Habitat	Northern coniferous forests.
Range	Alaska east to Newfoundland; sporadically seen in the northern border states in winter.

Northern Saw-whet Owl *Aegolius acadicus*

The fairly common Northern Saw-whet Owl is a close kin and look-alike of the rare Boreal Owl (see page 154). The Saw-whet, however, because of its more southerly distribution, is seen regularly throughout much of the United States. In the East, it is the smallest owl species. Well known as a strictly nocturnal hunter, it spends the day well hidden at its favorite roost. The Saw-whet also has a reputation for tameness. Like many of its brethren, it often makes its presence known by its characteristic calls.

Identification 7–8½". A small owl that lacks ear tufts and has yellow eyes and a dark bill. It is overall brown above; underparts are streaked with rufous markings. Juveniles are buff below.

Voice Simple, repeated whistles like those of a songflute; also a harsh, rasping call, likened to the whetting of a saw.

Habitat Coniferous and mixed forests, bogs, and wooded swamps.

Range Southern Alaska, southern Canada, and the northern U.S. Migratory. Found southward in winter, except in the southeastern and Gulf Coast states.

Birds of Prey
in Flight

Birds of Prey in Flight

While perched, raptors will usually display key field marks, but birds of prey are just as often seen in flight, particularly at migration junctures. At such times, overall size, shape, proportion, and flight behavior become more important than specific field marks as clues to identification.

Types of Flight

There are a number of aspects of flight behavior to observe. Birds in flight have different silhouettes depending on exactly what they are doing. When soaring, or circling on the rising heat of thermals, a hawk flies with its wing and tail feathers fully spread. It appears quite different when it is gliding, or flying without flapping. A glide usually involves pulling the wings and tail partially closed. Powered flight, the direct-line flight obtained through vigorous flapping, imparts yet a different appearance to the hawk.

Buteos

Buteos are large, long- and wide-winged raptors, commonly seen circling over open habitats or riding updrafts adjacent to mountain ridges. All move slowly, in wide circles, with little flapping of their wings. In level flight, their wingbeats are relatively slow and deep.

Swainson's Hawk

Swainson's Hawk Swainson's Hawk is the longest- and thinnest-winged of the buteos, and it shows a long tail. These features combine to make this species sometimes resemble a harrier or falcon. When soaring, it holds its wings in a distinct V shape (or dihedral) above the body. In a glide, its inner wing is thrust forward past the head, and the outer wing is pulled back deeply, giving a unique shape. In light morph birds, look for contrasting dark flight feathers.

Red-tailed Hawk The buteo most likely to be seen throughout North America is the Red-tailed Hawk. It is large, with a wingspan over four feet, and has a short tail. It soars on wide, flat or slightly raised wings. Seen from below it is light-colored (although there is a dark morph), and a belly-band is usually present. It flies with a deep flap; that is, its wings flap strongly, moving well below and above the body.

Broad-winged Hawk The smallest of the buteos, the Broad-winged Hawk has wings that are not noticeably broad. It holds the wings perpendicular to the body, and the outer portion of the wings is usually swept back enough in a soar to appear pointed, or shaped like a candle flame. When the bird glides,

Red-tailed Hawk

it pulls its wings back, giving it a falcon-like appearance. The wings also droop below the body in a glide.

Red-shouldered Hawk The Red-shouldered Hawk usually soars with flat wings that are thrust slightly forward. (The Red-tail holds its wings perpendicular to the body.) The wingtips often look squared off. Their flap is more shallow, stiff, and less powerful than in the Red-tailed Hawk. Adults' barred wings and tails are usually easily seen. These birds almost always show a "window" in the outer wing, at the base of the primaries. This is a patch that appears light in color due to translucent areas in the feathers.

Rough-legged Hawk The Rough-legged Hawk also shows long, thin wings and a long tail in flight. Of the buteos discussed here, only Rough-legs and Red-tails hover and kite (hold their wings motionless in the wind). The Rough-leg usually displays a contrasting wing pattern: a black patch on the underwing; a belly-band; and a white tail base. It soars with wings held above the body in a V not as distinct as the V of the Swainson's Hawk. The wings make a deep flap, but the flight appears less powerful than that of the Red-tailed Hawk.

Red-shouldered Hawk

Ferruginous Hawk	The largest buteo, the Ferruginous Hawk is usually very pale below, with a pale tail. Its wing flap is heavy, like that of an eagle, and it rides low over western ridge tops in a hunting style similar to that of the Golden Eagle. It soars and glides with wings held in a dihedral. A white patch on the outer upperwing is always visible, even in dark-morph individuals.
Osprey	The Osprey is not a buteo, but it is most likely to be confused with either the Rough-legged Hawk or the Ferruginous Hawk. It hovers and is very white below, but shows a contrasting wing pattern. It soars with inner wings raised and outer wings drooped, creating an M shape. In a glide, its inner wings are thrust far forward while the outer wings are swept back, showing a distinctive shape . The Osprey often appears more gull-like than hawk-like.
Accipiters	Accipiters are forest-dwellers with short, wide wings and long tails. They soar well, but usually their direct flight consists of a combination of flapping and gliding. These birds are highly aggressive and skilled at maneuvering; all of them feed on other birds.

Osprey

Sharp-shinned Hawk	The accipiter most likely seen in the East is the Sharp-shinned Hawk. It is quite small and uses a rapid "flap-flap-flap-glide" style in direct flight. In a soar it shows a small head, with wings thrust forward, and usually a squared tail. Immatures appear dirty brown below due to diffuse streaking.
Cooper's Hawk	The crow-sized Cooper's Hawk is the accipiter most likely to be seen in the West. It relies more on thermals than the Sharp-shinned Hawk. In a soar it shows a large head and perpendicular wings; that is, the leading edges of the wings form a perfectly straight line. It has a long, rounded, plume-like tail. Immatures are usually much lighter below than Sharp-shinneds, with a dark head and chest contrasting with the light belly.
Northern Goshawk	The Northern Goshawk is a very buteo-like accipiter, more likely to be confused with a Red-shouldered Hawk than with a Cooper's Hawk. It is very large; females are as large as a Red-tailed Hawk. While adults with gray and white plumage are unmistakable, immatures are a challenge to identify. A Northern Goshawk has a broad, wide, heavily banded tail.

Sharp-shinned Hawk

Its wings show bulging secondaries, a wing shape more similar to that of Sharp-shinned Hawks than of Cooper's Hawks.

Northern Harrier While not an accipiter, the Northern Harrier is more similar in shape (with its long, wide tail) and behavior (using low, maneuverable flight) to accipiters than to other raptors. Harriers have a distinctive, low, tilting flight over marshes and fields, and a white rump that is unmistakable. During migration, however, they fly higher and can appear very accipiter-like or falcon-like. Immatures look very dark, both on wings and body. Adult males are white below and gray above.

Falcons The falcons are rapid-flying raptors of open fields, prairies, plains, marshes, and coasts. They have long, pointed wings and can soar well, but they are more likely to use rapid, direct-flapping flight, gliding much less than accipiters do.

American Kestrel The American Kestrel is a small, Mourning-dove–sized raptor. It is by far the most commonly seen falcon, often sitting on power lines along roads, and it is the only North

Northern Harrier

American falcon that hovers. In flight, the male's bright red tail is distinctive; the female has a warm-brown banded tail. Seen overhead, this bird shows translucent spotting on the trailing edge of the wing. In a glide or powered flight, its wings are swept back gently.

Merlin The Merlin is identifiable by its low, very fast powered flight. Females and immatures are dark enough to show virtually no patterns at a distance; males are blue-gray above and tawny below. The wings are short, wide, and stubby compared to those of the kestrel. They move in rapid, stiff, shallow-pumping beats. In a glide or powered flight, the wings are swept back in hard angles.

Peregrine Falcon The size of the Peregrine Falcon is variable: Some males appear relatively small, and some females seem huge. Immatures appear very dark, like Merlins, while adult males can appear almost white below and pale gray above. Peregrines display a very powerful direct flight, with deep, rapid wingbeats, but their very flexible wings recall the flight of a loon or a cormorant. These falcons soar long and well, showing a distinctive pointed-wing silhouette, with

American Kestrel

wings held perpendicular to the body. Their shape in flight resembles that of an anchor or crossbow in the sky.

Prairie Falcon   The Prairie Falcon is a western specialty. It is very pale compared to the Peregrine, but has a distinctive dark underwing. Its fast, rapid direct flight is usually low. The wings are slightly less pointed than those of the Peregrine, with the wingbeats usually stiffer. It resembles a large Kestrel in having gently swept-back wings.

Gyrfalcon   Female Gyrfalcons are massive; small males overlap Peregrines in size. This bird is very rare in the contiguous 48 states, and difficult to identify; familiarity with the similar Peregrine and Northern Goshawk is helpful. The Gyrfalcon's low, rapid hunting flight brings to mind a giant Merlin. Deceptively fast, it seems to cover ground without flapping. Its wing flap is shallow, done mostly with the outer wing. Gyrfalcons of all plumages should show translucent flight feathers below, unlike Peregrines. They have long, wide tails and comparatively short wings.

Prairie Falcon

Kites   Kites are medium-sized raptors with relatively long wings and tails. Graceful and buoyant fliers, more at home in the air than on a perch, kites are often seen gliding and soaring over their hunting territories throughout the daylight hours. The following descriptions apply to the three species of kites that are regularly migratory, and therefore most likely to be seen away from their immediate breeding areas. The White-tailed, Mississippi, and Swallow-tailed kites all have long, pointed wings that give them a distinctive falcon-like appearance. (See text descriptions for details on the paddle-winged Snail and Hook-billed kites.)

White-tailed Kite   The White-tailed Kite has pointed, falcon-like wings but a distinctive white-tailed, black-shouldered plumage. In behavior, it is very similar to the American Kestrel, hunting from perches and hovering frequently. It uses a variety of flight patterns but soars, glides, and flaps with wings held in a marked dihedral.

Mississippi Kite   The smallest and most falcon-like of north American kites is the Mississippi Kite. The adult's pale head and body, dark wings, and black tail are distinctive, but dark immatures

White-tailed Kite

and subadults can appear very similar to the Peregrine in shape. This kite's slow, deep, stiff flap differs from that of the Peregrine. In a full soar, it can appear much like a Broad-winged Hawk, with pointed wings; however, a long, splayed tail generally can be seen.

American Swallow-tailed Kite

Unmistakable, with its deeply forked tail, the American Swallow-tailed Kite could perhaps be confused only with an immature frigatebird. However, when in the Swallow-tail's range, careful birdwatchers check all distant white-bellied birds assumed to be Osprey, because the Swallow-tail is nearly Osprey-sized and shows similarly swept-back wings. Its flight is often very low and amazingly slow; the "swallow tails" act as airfoils, allowing what appears to be slow-motion flight.

Vultures and Eagles

In many aspects of their biology, the New World vultures are distinctly different from the eagles, falcons, and hawks with which they are regularly associated. Several aspects of vulture behavior, however, are similar to that of diurnal raptors. In particular, the vultures' soaring flight, whether it be on their daily scavenging expeditions or on migrations, is

American Swallow-tailed Kite

virtually identical to the flight of most hawks. In fact, throughout most of the United States, a hawk watcher seeing a large, dark, soaring bird is just as likely to be watching a vulture as a hawk. With practice, however, distinctions between hawks and vultures in flight become apparent.

Turkey Vulture
The Turkey Vulture is a large, nearly eagle-sized bird with a long tail and small head. When soaring, its wings are held at a fairly steep angle above the body. The characteristic contrast between the flight feathers and coverts disappears with distance and in bad light. Turkey Vultures seldom flap once aloft, but rather soar and glide with constant tilting, rocky motions that cause them to appear unsteady. This occurs in both heavy and light winds. A distant black bird with a rocking flight and wings held in a dihedral is assuredly a Turkey Vulture.

Black Vulture
The Black Vulture is considerably smaller than the Turkey Vulture—not much larger than a Red-tailed Hawk. The white in its wing is confined to the wingtips and is visible from above and below. The tail is very short, making the

Turkey Vulture

180

bird appear almost tailless in a full soar. This vulture uses a rapid, choppy, laborious flap when gaining altitude, but once aloft it often soars higher than the Turkey Vulture. Black Vultures soar in pairs, their wings held flat or in a slight dihedral.

Crested Caracara   Actually a member of the falcon family, the Crested Caracara is by plumage, shape, and behavior most closely allied with the vultures and eagles. It exhibits a powerful direct flight with medium-deep, slow wingbeats. When soaring, it shows the body shape of a Bald Eagle, the tail of a Golden Eagle, and the wing pattern of the Black Vulture, soaring on flat wings and gliding with wings slightly drooped.

Bald Eagle   Adult Bald Eagles are unmistakable, but immatures are highly variable. Adults have large heads, necks, and bills and relatively short tails. They soar on wings held flat or in a slight dihedral. The plank-like wings have parallel leading and trailing edges. The Bald Eagle has powerful direct flight; it flaps with wings largely held above its body, perhaps in an adaptation for its low hunting flights over water.

Bald Eagle

Golden Eagle In contrast to Bald Eagles, Golden Eagles show small
heads, necks, and bills, and comparatively longer tails. Their
flap is more hawk-like than the vulture-like flap of a Bald
Eagle, and they soar with wings held in a significant
dihedral. Bulging secondaries and wings pinched in at the
body give a different soaring shape than that of the Bald
Eagle, with leading and trailing edges not parallel.
Immatures have white tails with dark tips; on the
underwing, white is confined to the flight feathers on the
outer wings. In the Bald Eagle, the white is concentrated at
the "armpit" at the base of the wing on the coverts, not on
the flight feathers.

Golden Eagle

Parts of a Bird

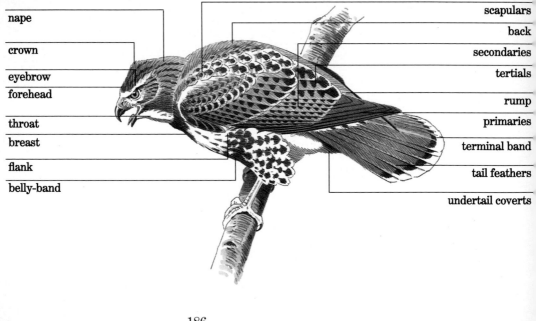

nape

crown

eyebrow

forehead

throat

breast

flank

belly-band

scapulars

back

secondaries

tertials

rump

primaries

terminal band

tail feathers

undertail coverts

Glossary

Accidental
(See Vagrant.)

Aerie
A nest on a cliff or mountaintop.

Coverts
The small feathers covering the bases of other, usually larger, feathers. Coverts provide a smooth, aerodynamic surface.

Eye-ring
A fleshy or feathered ring around the eye.

Eye-stripe
A stripe running horizontally from the base of the bill through the eye.

Flight feathers
The long feathers of the wing and tail used for flight. The flight feathers of the wing are comprised of primaries, secondaries, and tertials.

Kite
To fly holding the wings motionless in the wind (verb). Also, a medium-sized raptor with long wings and a long tail (noun).

Mandible
One of the two parts (upper and lower) of a bird's bill.

Mantle
The back and the upper surfaces of the wings.

Morph
One of two or more distinct color types within the same species, occurring independently of age, sex, season, and geography. Also referred to as phase.

Phase
(See Morph.)

Race
(See Subspecies.)

Spicule
A minute, spikelike body on the

pads of the toes of some birds of prey.

Stoop
To fly or dive down quickly to attack prey.

Subspecies
A geographical population that is slightly different from other populations of the same species. Also called a race.

Vagrant
A bird that occurs outside its normal range. Also referred to as accidental.

Wing bar
A bar of contrasting color on the upper wing coverts.

Wing lining
A collective term for the coverts of the underwing.

Wing stripe
A lengthwise stripe on the upper surface of the extended wing.

Hawk-watching Organizations

Large numbers of hawks can be seen during migratory periods in spring and fall. Concentrations occur along mountain ridges, such as on Hawk Mountain in Pennsylvania, or along the coasts. Peninsulas such as Cape May, New Jersey, attract vast raptor concentrations; often thousands may be seen in a single day. Other concentrations are found in the Florida Keys, South Texas, along the Great Lakes, and on the Pacific Coast north of San Francisco. Ridge flights occur in both eastern and western North America.

To obtain specific information on hawk-watching opportunities, contact the organizations listed here.

The Cape May Bird Observatory
P. O. Box 3, Cape May Point
New Jersey 08212
(609) 884-2736
(Spring and fall flights)

Hawk Mountain Sanctuary Association
R.R. 2, Box 191, Kempton
Pennsylvania 19529-9449
(215) 756-6961
(Fall flights)

Braddock Bay Raptor Research
432 Manitou Beach Road
Hilton, New York 14468
(Rochester area; spring flights)

Hawk Ridge Nature Reserve
Duluth Audubon Society
c/o UMD Biology Department
Duluth, Minnesota 55812
(Fall flights)

Hawkwatch International
P. O. Box 35706, Albuquerque
New Mexico 87176-5706
(Western states; spring and fall locations)

Golden Gate Raptor Observatory
Building 201, Fort Mason
San Francisco, California 94123
(Fall flights)

For additional information on annual hawk flights, and for the location of the hawk watch nearest you, write:

The Hawk Migration Association of North America, Inc.
c/o Myriam Moore, Secretary
32 Columbia Avenue
Lynchburg, Virginia 24503

Index

Credits

Photographers

Ron Austing (51, 61, 125)
Robert A. Behrstock/
Naturewide Images (139)
Steve Bentsen (33)
Fred Bruemmer (119)
Gay Bumgarner (147)
Robert D. Campbell (121)
William S. Clark (63, 77, 111)
Sharon Cummings (143)
Rob Curtis/The Early Birder (89)
Richard Day (167)

DEMBINSKY PHOTO ASSOCIATES:
SharkSong, M. Kazmers (43)
Skip Moody (131)
Stan Osolinski (27)

Jack Dermid (73, 181)
Jon Farrar (75)
John Hendrickson (85, 95, 145)
Greg Homel/Natural
Elements, Inc. (69, 87)
Robert Y. Kaufman/Yogi, Inc. (133)
Steve Kaufman (front cover)
G. C. Kelley (141)

Wayne Lankinen (155)
Harold Lindstrom (135)
Steffan Mittelhauser (153)
C. Allan Morgan (65, 83)
Teruaki Morioka (47, 49)
Arthur & Elaine Morris/
Birds As Art (23, 53, 55, 157)

PHOTO/NATS, INC.:
Jennifer A. Loomis (151)
Sam Fried (123, 127, 129)

Ron Planck (149)
Ron Sanford (18-19, 45)
Johann Schumacher Design
(3, 57, 158-159)
Ervio Sian (91)
Hugh P. Smith, Jr. (81)
Mitchell D. Smith (21, 109)
Charles G. Summers, Jr.
(113, 183)
Clay Sutton (179)
Frank S. Todd (25)
Tom J. Ulrich (99, 105, 115,
117, 185)
Larry West (71)
Brian Wheeler/VIREO (31, 79, 101)
Brian Wheeler (29, 35, 37, 39, 41,

67, 93, 97, 161, 163, 165, 169, 171,
173, 175, 177)
Dale & Marian Zimmerman
(59, 103)
Paul Zimmerman (107)
Tim Zurowski (137)

Cover Photograph: Snowy Owl
by Steve Kaufman
Title Page: Peregrine Falcon by
Tom J. Ulrich
Spread (pp. 18–19): Bald Eagles
by Ron Sanford
Spread (pp. 158–159): Northern
Harrier by Johann Schumacher
Design

Illustrators

Range maps by Paul Singer
Drawing (186) by Barry Van
Dusen
Silhouette drawings by
Douglas Pratt and Paul Singer

Staff

This book was created by
Chanticleer Press.
All editorial inquiries should
be addressed to:
Chanticleer Press
568 Broadway, Suite #1005A
New York, NY 10012
(212) 941-1522

Chanticleer Press Staff
Founding Publisher:
Paul Steiner
Publisher: Andrew Stewart
Managing Editor: Edie Locke
Production Manager:
Deirdre Duggan Ventry
Assistant to the Publisher:
Kelly Beekman
Text Editor: Carol M. Healy
Consultant: John Farrand, Jr.
Photo Editor: Lori J. Hogan
Designer: Sheila Ross
Research Assistant:
Debora Diggins

Original series design by
Massimo Vignelli.

To purchase this book or other
National Audubon Society
illustrated nature books, please
contact:
Alfred A. Knopf, Inc.
201 East 50th Street
New York, NY 10022
(800) 733-3000